GEMINI

GEMINI

22 May–21 June

PATTY GREENALL & CAT JAVOR

Printed exclusively for Restoration Hardware

An Hachette Livre UK Company

First published in Great Britain in 2004 by
Spruce, a division of Octopus Publishing Group Ltd
2–4 Heron Quays, London E14 4JP.
www.octopusbooks.co.uk

Copyright © Octopus Publishing Group Ltd 2004, 2008
Text copyright © Patty Greenall and Cat Javor 2004, 2008

Distributed in the United States and Canada by
Hachette Book Group USA
237 Park Avenue
New York
NY 10017

Patty Greenall and Cat Javor assert their moral
rights to be identified as the authors of this book.

Illustrations: Gerry Baptist

ISBN 13: 978-1-84601-303-4
ISBN 10: 1-846-01303-8

Printed and bound in China

10 9 8 7 6 5 4 3 2 1

WHAT IS **ASTROLOGY?**

Astrology is the practice of interpreting the positions and movements of celestial bodies with regard to what they can tell us about life on Earth. In particular it is the study of the cycles of the Sun, Moon, and the planets of our solar system, and their journeys through the twelve signs of the zodiac—Aries, Taurus, Gemini, Cancer, Leo, Virgo, Libra, Scorpio, Sagittarius, Capricorn, Aquarius, and Pisces—all of which provide astrologers with a rich diversity of symbolic information and meaning.

Astrology has been labeled a science, an occult magical practice, a religion, and an art, yet it cannot be confined by any one of these descriptions. Perhaps the best way to describe it is as an evolving tradition.

Throughout the world, for as far back as history can inform us, people have been looking up at the skies and attaching stories and meanings to what they see there. Neolithic peoples in Europe built huge stone structures such as Stonehenge in southern England in order to plot the cycles of the Sun and Moon, cycles that were so important to a fledgling agricultural society. There are star-lore traditions in the ancient cultures of India, China, South America, and Africa, and among the indigenous people of Australia. The ancient Egyptians plotted the rising of the star Sirius, which marked the annual flooding of the Nile, and in ancient Babylon, astronomer-priests would perform astral divination in the service of their king and country.

Since its early beginnings, astrology has grown, changed, and diversified into a huge body of knowledge that has been added to by many learned men and women throughout history. It has continued to evolve and become richer and more informative, despite periods when it went out of favor because of religious, scientific, and political beliefs.

Offering us a deeper knowledge of ourselves, a profound insight into what motivates, inspires, and, in some cases, hinders, our ability to be truly our authentic selves, astrology equips us better to make the choices and decisions that confront us daily. It is a wonderful tool, which can be applied to daily life and our understanding of the world around us.

The horoscope—or birth chart—is the primary tool of the astrologer and the position of the Sun, Moon, Mercury, Venus, Mars, Jupiter, Saturn,

Uranus, Neptune, and Pluto at the moment a person was born are all considered when one is drawn up. Each planet has its own domain, affinities, and energetic signature, and the aspects or relationships they form to each other when plotted on the horoscope reveal a fascinating array of information. The birth, or Sun, sign is the sign of the zodiac that the Sun was passing through at the time of birth. The energetic signature of the Sun is concerned with a person's sense of uniqueness and self-esteem. To be a vital and creative individual is a fundamental need, and a person's Sun sign represents how that need most happily manifests in that person. This is one of the most important factors taken into account by astrologers. Each of the twelve Sun signs has a myriad of ways in which it can express its core meaning. The more a person learns about their individual Sun sign, the more they can express their own unique identity.

ZODIAC WHEEL

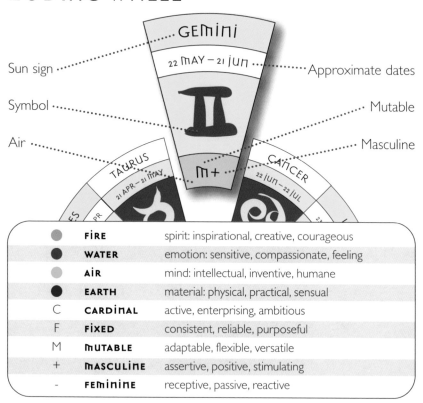

Sun sign

Symbol

Air

GEMINI

22 MAY – 21 JUN

TAURUS
21 APR – 21 MAY

CANCER
22 JUN – 22 JUL

M+

Approximate dates

Mutable

Masculine

●	**FIRE**	spirit: inspirational, creative, courageous
●	**WATER**	emotion: sensitive, compassionate, feeling
●	**AIR**	mind: intellectual, inventive, humane
●	**EARTH**	material: physical, practical, sensual
C	**CARDINAL**	active, enterprising, ambitious
F	**FIXED**	consistent, reliable, purposeful
M	**MUTABLE**	adaptable, flexible, versatile
+	**MASCULINE**	assertive, positive, stimulating
-	**FEMININE**	receptive, passive, reactive

PART ONE

THE ESSENTIAL
Gemini

RULERSHİPS

Gemini is the third sign of the zodiac, the first of the Air signs, and is ruled by the planet Mercury. Its symbol is the Twins—a human rather than animal symbol—who represent intellect, social contact, and communication. There are earthly correspondences of everything in life for each of the Sun signs. The parts of the human body that Gemini represents are the arms and hands. Gemstones for Gemini are agate, marcasite, and alexandrite, which changes from red to green depending on whether it's viewed in natural or artificial light. Gemini is a Masculine and Mutable sign. It signifies hills, mountains, and places used for storage, books, cars, short journeys, mail, communication, writers, newspapers, gossip and chatting, as well as butterflies, monkeys, and mice, tansy, vervain, woodbine, and yarrow.

THESE ARE SOME OF THE TRADITIONAL ASSOCIATIONS OF

GEMINI

The parts of the human body that Gemini
represents are the arms and hands.

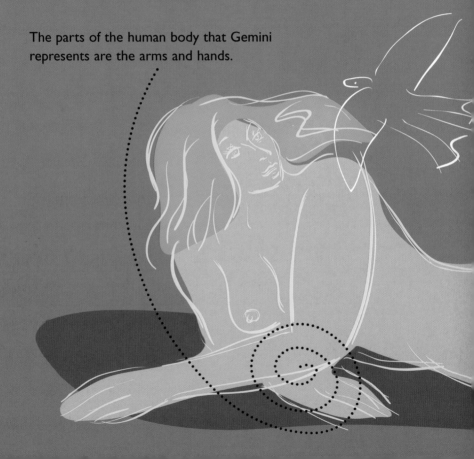

Books, cars, short journeys

-iters, newspapers

butterflies

PERSONALITY

Those born under the sign of the Twins often seem to be two separate, individual characters rolled into one. Astrologically, Gemini is described as one of the "bicorporeal," or double-bodied signs, which is why they are said to have a dualistic nature. Thus they behave differently depending on the perspective they happen to adopt at any given moment. Perhaps a better way to describe them might be "multi-faceted," like a gemstone fashioned to reflect the light from many angles. They are versatile, adaptable, and utterly fascinating when you see them change, chameleon-like, from one opinion to the next. It can get incredibly confusing, even infuriating, for people who want to pin them down, for those born under Gemini seem to hold an opinion very strongly at one moment but the next time the subject comes up for discussion, they may take the opposite point of view and argue it just as powerfully.

Geminis are excellent at debate but it's best to avoid getting into discussion with them if you're not adept at verbal twisting and turning. Their oral skills are often described as "verbal gymnastics." Anyone with a point to make would have an enormous advantage with a Gemini on their side. It's not that they seek argument or wish to win; they simply enjoy banter and expect others to enjoy it, too. In fact, they never tire of conversation, however intense, and they don't mind losing an argument—though they rarely do.

One of the worst accusations frequently thrown at Geminis is that they are liars or twisters of the truth. But if they are, it's not their fault! Their planetary ruler, Mercury, "the wing-footed messenger of the gods," was known as "the trickster." Astronomically, the planet Mercury is close enough to Earth to be visible, but it is elusive—sometimes you can see it and sometimes you can't. This is due to a number of factors, including how close Mercury is to the Sun. In addition, Mercury rules quicksilver—a metal that glitters and is scintillating, yet is also capable of rolling away in a flash. All of this helps to explain why Geminis appear to be so changeable, but when they are saying something, they truly believe in what they are saying—except of course when they are being deliberately mischievous and tricky! But the problem is, who can say what they will believe tomorrow? When they do change their point of view, their defense is to say that the world is changing and we are constantly learning new things, so how can anyone stick stubbornly to one opinion?

The god Mercury was also the inventor of language and Gemini's language skills are so developed that they are usually very good at imitating and learning foreign tongues. They are quick learners, too, and are also able to pass on information to anyone who missed it the first time around, but they are not often known for their patience when doing so! Anyone who spends too long pondering a point will be left far behind. Geminis are always eager to move onto a new subject and quench their thirst for information.

Their mental agility is remarkable; everything interests them—at least until the next thing catches their attention. Even when they're talking at top speed, which they often are, their brain is working on at least three other things at the same time. They see patterns and make connections between disparate subjects that would baffle mere mortals of slower intellect.

Geminis adore lively debates and clever comedic comments and generally make wonderful conversationalists, full of witty repartee and brilliant banter. They seem to have something to say on every subject, even if it's only to ask interesting questions of those who possess a deeper knowledge of the topic under discussion. In fact, if there is just one thing they are passionate about, it is communicating their ideas and, of course, they are very good at doing this. They are clever, articulate, stimulating, and titillating, and there is rarely an uncomfortable silence in their company. No party would be complete without a lively Gemini!

The other side of the coin is that Geminis possess very little patience and have the boredom threshold of a two-year-old. Thankfully, though, they are genuinely sweet and good-natured enough to remain cheerful and friendly as they extricate themselves from dull, mundane conversations that have failed to hold their interest. They would hate to think that anything they have said or done has caused upset and hurt. That would only bring them feelings of remorse, which they'd find difficult to cope with. They much prefer keeping everything bright and breezy, and light and easy, so they are rarely ever caught being deliberately rude. In fact, they can make excellent diplomats; they are never short of something to say and have an excellent sense of humor, which usually puts others immediately at ease.

If a thing is truly fresh, new, and exciting it will appeal to Gemini thrill-seekers, who are not known for their ability to sit still for long periods of time. They are always out and about somewhere on an errand or keeping to their busy schedules. They are busy people with particularly dexterous hands. If they aren't writing an article, letter, or email, they will be tapping their fingers, chewing their nails, or playing an instrument. They are of a nervous disposition and are constantly searching for intriguing subjects that will challenge their understanding. Since they frequently use their arms and hands to accompany their words, gesticulating is a true Gemini trait.

CAREER & MONEY

The work arena is where Geminis really stand out. Being so adaptable means that they are capable of just about anything. They are the jack-of-all-trades par excellence and it's this gift of versatility that brings them success. For them, anything is possible and the sky is their limit. Any company would gain by having a Gemini as an employee. Because of their dualistic nature, they can handle more than one thing at a time and they are fast learners and quick doers. They are efficient, productive, and interested in whatever they choose to do, so they get the job done in half the time that anyone else would take. So, what do they do in all that spare time? They can't tolerate idleness, so if they're not given something to do, they'll find something. At best, like an in-house cheerleader, they'll be encouraging their colleagues to work and giving everyone pep talks. This might be irritating, but only to those who can't keep up! At worst, they'll be the ones playing games on their computer or telephone handset, or they might be found in the company chat room. But they can't really be reprimanded for taking a break during company time. After all, they will have fulfilled their requirements!

If they're the boss, then it's another story altogether. Being in charge is not so much a problem for Geminis as for those who work for them. It's not easy to match their pace and follow their bullet train of thought. To those who take time to grasp a new concept, the Gemini boss, with his or her convoluted thought processes, can seem all over the place. But similarly-minded "brainiacs" who can follow Gemini's flashes of brilliance, will share in the glory, as long as they don't get sidetracked in the process.

Geminis are natural salespeople, whether they are talking themselves into a high-powered position or talking someone else into buying something that they don't need. They know just how to persuade people, whether they're selling a car or an idea. Their talent for forward-thinking enables them to be one step ahead when dealing with any objections people might make, and they are also usually one step ahead when it comes to the world of technology. They make superb writers, journalists, reporters, pre-school and elementary teachers, secretaries, messengers, merchants, and mathematicians. They are multi-talented and know just how to get what they want.

As far as money is concerned, Geminis are just as capable of making a fortune as anyone, but however much money they have, their bank balance does seem to fluctuate more than other people's. This is perhaps because they are not afraid of taking the occasional risk; sometimes they win, sometimes they lose. In any case, their ability to move on means that they don't waste any time clinging to the past. What they need, though, is a bit of persistence and staying power. If they can combine these with their superior thinking skills, then the world will be their oyster.

THE GEMINI CHILD

The contrariness of Gemini children is recognizable from the moment these bright little sparks come into the world. When mom and pop want them to sleep, they'll want to play. When it's time to eat, they'll want to sleep, and when it's time to play in the baby gym, they'll cry with hunger. And just when mom and pop have adapted their routine to suit their little one, the Gemini baby will revert to the original one. When they begin to walk and talk, which they'll do quicker than most other children, they'll be impossible to pin down. It can seem as if they're in two places at once—a legacy of being born under the sign of the Twins. One second they're sitting looking at a book and the next, they've taken everything out of the kitchen cabinets. Gemini children are on a voyage of discovery; everything that catches their attention needs further investigation. Their inquiring little minds require constant stimulation and since they see stimulation everywhere, they have to go everywhere in order to get it.

Gemini children are always asking, "Why?" but they don't hang around long enough to hear the answer. This can be a major problem when it comes to their education. They're usually very adept at learning to read and write, but once they have grasped the basics, they won't stick at it to get the depth and the details. Yet they're naturally so clever that they somehow just seem to muddle through without their teachers noticing that there might be a gap somewhere in their learning.

The Gemini child's cheerful friendliness and vivid imagination mean that they're often popular playmates and have a wide circle of friends. But as they move into puberty and adolescence, their active, alert, and frequently changing mind can become something of a burden since they find it difficult to make a decision. This can lead to moody, sulky, and deliberately contrary behavior unless they are helped to see that it's often better to make a positive start to something and adapt to circumstances along the way, rather than endlessly debate all the options in their minds and end up doing nothing. But having these lighthearted, fun-loving children around is a joy. They are so full of life that they have a way of keeping even the determinedly staid young at heart.

PERFECT GIFTS

Choosing a gift for a Gemini is something of a hit-or-miss affair. It's difficult to predict what will work for them. Any gift needs to fascinate them and captivate their eternally youthful, active minds. They will love something sassy and scintillating, but buying the latest gadget won't guarantee success because chances are, they have already been there, done it, and bought the t-shirt.

However, since Gemini is ruled by Mercury, the planet of communications, a gift that helps them to keep in touch with others or that is related to information should fit the bill. When it comes to clothing, keep in mind that Gemini rules the arms and hands, so think gloves, rings, a trendy watch, or an armful of bangles. For Lady Gemini, a manicure set or selection of nail varnishes will always please, while books, pens, and stationery will make any Gemini happy. If you're looking for something a bit more special, an ever-changing lava lamp or a radio-controlled vehicle will bring a smile to a Gemini's face and a game or puzzle will hold their attention—for at least a day! What to avoid? Presents that don't do anything. They're sure to end up in the charity shop.

FAVORITE **FOODS**

Variety is the spice of life for the Gemini palate. What they crave one day certainly won't appeal the next. Sure, they'll have their favorite dishes, but they'd rather eat them on a strict rotation with at least two days of new, different flavors in between, before returning to the old favorites and rediscovering them all over again. It's impossible to work out what will tickle their tastebuds from one moment to the next, and indeed, they never know themselves. At the dinner table, Geminis chat so much that they often don't even taste their food or notice what they're putting into their mouths. But they do seem to have a good natural instinct about nutrition and often reach for the very food their body needs at the moment it needs it.

The other thing about Geminis is how their appetite can vary. At one meal they can eat and eat until not another morsel can pass their lips; at another, they'll pick like a bird, taking just one taste of everything, then putting their cutlery down with a satisfied sigh having eaten little more than a few mouthfuls.

Geminis usually love their cereal in the morning, but if they don't have time to sit and eat, they'll happily grab a pre-packaged snack to eat on the run. Of course, the best pre-packaged foods are those that Mother Nature herself packs, so you'll often find a piece of fruit in the pocket or bag of a gadabout Gemini. They particularly like to eat at restaurants that offer "mezze-style" dining—lots of small, spicy dishes with unusual flavors that will cater to their need for variety.

FASHION & STYLE

"Mix 'n' match" is the catchphrase that suits the Gemini sense of style. They will very rarely be seen wearing the same outfit twice, preferring to ring the changes with different combinations of shirts and slacks or skirts until it seems as though they have the most extensive wardrobe in town. Remember, Gemini is clever! And this extends to their choice of clothes, too. They get bored with their clothes just as quickly as they get bored with everything else, which is why there's a dash of the faddish follower-of-fashion about them. They like to know what the latest trend is and to wear it, but they are clever at adapting it into a "seen here first" style statement, which, of course, they never wear again in quite the same way. When they're young, this can lead to their having an endless array of inexpensive garments that stay on their backs for about as long as fashion magazines stay on bookstore shelves. However, as they get older, Geminis often become shrewder about how to cater to their need for a fresh new look, without having to head out shopping every five minutes.

Whatever the fashion, season or choice of fabric, Gemini colors always have a light, spring-like feel to them. Even if they are wearing a darker, more muted color, or even black, Geminis will look best if they offset their outfit with at least one crisp, bright item to lift the look and prevent it becoming heavy and drab. White and yellow are excellent choices: sky blues and fresh pinks are perfect.

IDEAL HOMES

The Gemini home is, in a word, busy. It's not so much that Geminis are always on the move—well, they do tend to be active—more that their homes are like Grand Central Station. There's a great deal of coming and going—people meeting up, minds converging, friends chattering, and information being exchanged—and all simultaneously. Surprisingly, Gemini people tend to keep their homes tidy, with everything in its place. They have to, or home would become a confusion of paperwork, receipts, messages, instruction manuals, and the like.

Their home is comfortable, but not in a homey way. It's more like a hotel room—somewhere with all the amenities and comforts anyone would want for a short stay. It's a sleek, clean place where all are welcome, however it doesn't suit everyone as it doesn't encourage a sense of restfulness. Geminis need rest and sleep like anyone else, but they don't need a lot of comfort. With their eager curiosity about new things and new places, as well as their short attention span, they could live just about anywhere!

PART TWO

RISING SIGNS

WHAT IS A **RISING** SIGN?

Your rising sign is the zodiacal sign that could be seen rising on the eastern horizon at the time and place of your birth. Each sign takes about two and a half hours to rise — approximately one degree every four minutes. Because it is so fast moving, the rising sign represents a very personal part of the horoscope, so even if two people were born on the same day and year as one another, their different rising signs will make them very different people.

It is easier to understand the rising sign when the entire birth chart is seen as a circular map of the heavens. Imagine the rising sign — or ascendant — at the eastern point of the circle. Opposite is where the Sun sets — the descendant. The top of the chart is the part of the sky that is above, where the Sun reaches at midday, and the bottom of the chart is below, where the Sun would be at midnight. These four points divide the circle, or birth chart, into four. Those quadrants are then each divided into three, making a total of twelve, known as houses, each of which represents a certain aspect of life. Your rising sign corresponds to the first house and establishes which sign of the zodiac occupied each of the other eleven houses when you were born.

All of which makes people astrologically different from one another; not all Geminis are alike! The rising sign generally indicates what a person looks like. For instance, people with Leo, the sign of kings, rising, probably walk with a noble air and find that people often treat them like royalty. Those that have Pisces rising frequently have soft and sensitive looks and they might find that people are forever pouring their hearts out to them.

The rising sign is a very important part of the entire birth chart and should be considered in combination with the Sun sign and all the other planets!

THE RISING SIGNS FOR GEMINI

To work out your rising sign, you need to know your exact time of birth—if hospital records aren't available, try asking your family and friends. Now turn to the charts on pages 38–43. There are three charts, covering New York, Sydney, and London, all set to Greenwich Mean Time. Choose the correct chart for your place of birth and, if necessary, add or subtract the number of hours difference from GMT (for example, Sydney is approximately ten hours ahead, so you need to subtract ten hours from your time of birth). Then use a ruler to carefully find the point where your GMT time of birth meets your date of birth—this point indicates your rising sign.

GEMINI WITH ARIES RISING

Geminis born with Aries rising are academics right down to their fingertips. Even if they never liked school or any other form of institutionalized learning, they've been actively gathering information since the day they were born and filing it away in their enormously clever brain.

There is also a huge helping of the wheeler-dealer about them; they can spot an opportunity at a thousand paces and will be turning a profit on it before anyone else can say, "What a good idea!" These people notice everything and talk constantly about it with enthusiasm and verve. When Aries is rising, the Gemini native attacks life with energetic playfulness. Their wit is razor-sharp, but since they delight in the company of others so much, it would be unusual for them to use it to be deliberately cruel or unkind. Their observations hit the mark, but their heart is that of an innocent. They have an aura of eternal youth, no matter what their age, and always appear fresh and ready to take on new challenges, particularly those of an intellectual variety. Fun-loving to a fault and yet seriously interested in everyone and everything around them, these people are ambitious, courageous, and ingenious.

GEMINI WITH **TAURUS** RISING

The tenacity that comes with Taurus rising is a valuable commodity for Gemini individuals to possess. It is immediately apparent that not only do they have a quick and clever brain, they also have enough quiet determination to carry their brilliant ideas through to completion. These bright, sociable, and persevering people have practicality as well as ingenuity at their disposal and that makes for a very powerful combination, particularly when it comes to the gathering of wealth. There's the heart of a merchant beating in their chest, and even if they never go in for commerce, they know instinctively what the public desires. As lovers of art, beauty, and luxury themselves, they are creative on both an intellectual and a practical level. Although good communicators and as vociferous as other Geminis, those with Taurus rising prefer to take their time before saying what's on their mind. They have a lovely, sincere way of expressing themselves that often endears them to others and encourages confidence and trust. It might be that they enjoy the party scene a little too much, and indulge and get over-excited to the point where frequent periods of rest and recuperation are required, but that's less a fault, more an added attractive quality.

GEMINI WITH **GEMINI** RISING

When the already buzzy Gemini has Gemini rising, they just seem to vibrate with verve and enthusiasm. Like a battery-powered gymnast, they can do mental and physical backflips that leave the rest of humanity looking as though it has two left feet and a severe hangover. Graceful and dexterous, they are the ultimate multi-tasker, capable of having several irons in the fire while juggling balls and spinning plates. Geminis with Gemini rising are imaginative and inventive, ambitious and aspiring, and they never have enough informational input to satisfy their voracious intellectual appetites. They would make brilliant gossip columnists simply because they find absolutely everything and everyone fascinating, and, what's more, they're excellent raconteurs who find a funny twist to almost every story. Lighthearted and fun-loving, the Gemini with Gemini rising finds it almost impossible to get bogged down in anything so serious that it would quench their thirst for new and thrilling experiences. They're so restless and excitable that they can't stay in one place for long; there's always more to learn, more to investigate, and more pleasure to pursue. If on occasion they become anxious and highly strung—which is practically a given—then exhaustion could be the result, but their recuperative powers are as lightning-quick as their brilliant brain, so they'll soon be back to their old tricks.

GEMINI WITH **CANCER** RISING

The changeability of Gemini is accentuated when Cancer is rising, which is both a boon and a bane. With a change in the direction of the wind or with a new tide, there will always be a fresh opportunity and, because they are so clever and their instincts are so finely tuned, they'll always be able to spot it. From an early age, they learn that all things come in their own good time, but these individuals are so full of brilliant and ambitious ideas that they can hardly wait to get things moving. Mostly they are lucky in that they can adapt to any situation and deal with what life sends them while maintaining a cheery disposition and remaining consummately capable. Fond of home and family, they still find it possible to fit into any environment and are sociable, charming, and totally natural in their ability to reach out and engage the interest of everyone they meet. There's a powerful romantic streak in the Gemini with Cancer rising. They have a fertile imagination, making them masters of the art of spinning gossamer dreams, and they are witty and intelligent, yet seductive and alluring at the same time.

GEMINI WITH **LEO** RISING

♌ The nobility that Leo rising lends to the ingenious Gemini makes for an affectionate, kind-hearted soul with a wicked sense of humor and a dry, amusing wit. Quick to laugh and smile, these are outspoken, frank, and opinionated people who like nothing better than to find themselves surrounded by their many friends, sharing ideas, and throwing banter back and forth like a tennis ball. Charming and friendly, they thrive on the attention they receive for their brilliant observations and enlightened insights. There is a touch of the philosopher about them, as though they are in search of the brave new world that might be created from the wonderful ideas flashing around inside their heads—the reconstruction of anything that is drab, dull, or boring is something of a mission for them. They love life, and enjoy a dash of opulence and a generous helping of scintillating intellectual intrigue. They are more conscientious and dedicated in their pursuits than other Geminis, yet their minds are constantly open to new ideas and inspiration. They don't allow themselves to get bogged down in the petty and mundane; they have far loftier areas in which to distinguish themselves, and they often do just that.

GEMINI WITH **VIRGO** RISING

♍ The quick-thinking Gemini becomes more contemplative when Virgo is rising. This, of course, takes nothing away from their huge mental abilities for Virgo is also ruled by the planet Mercury. Virgo rising adds the benefits of industriousness and endurance, making them more skillful in the practice of their pursuits. Less quick to jump to conclusions and more conscientious in their approach to learning, Gemini with Virgo rising is a powerful combination when it comes to making a mark on the world. Academic and literary careers are not unheard of, but it is just as likely that their interests will take them into the business world where they can make a profitable impact. Lively yet modest, sweet yet wickedly witty, these Geminis are unassuming intellectuals par excellence. Their conversations are stimulating and informative, their observations measured and discriminating. They're fun to be around, can deliver a joke with perfect timing, and are supportive and helpful. They also have a fierce ambition to achieve mastery in whatever they turn their thoughts and hands to. They may be highly strung or nervous on occasion, but it's that energetic, edgy quality that assures their success in life.

GEMINI WITH **LIBRA** RISING

This is one of the most pleasing Geminis as they are usually very pleasant to look at and delightful to listen to. Libra rising adds a certain sweetness to the friendly, chatty Gemini. People respond very well to them, which is why they're so good-natured. Being fair-minded and having an uncanny sense of what other people want, make them perfect diplomats. They embrace love with an almost uncontrollable enthusiasm, so it's rare to find a Gemini with Libra rising who stays single for long. They love to love and they adore attention because they are natural show-offs, though in a charming way. They are cheerful, good-natured, and larger-than-life, and have a playful personality. They are highly creative and make fine actors and artists, and are also good with children. Whatever they do for a living should be an expression of their inner self—nothing mundane will do. They know what they want out of life and this is all-important to them. This is a Gemini who enjoys all the pleasures of life and knows how to live it to the full.

GEMINI WITH **SCORPIO** RISING

♏ The personal magnetism of Gemini with Scorpio rising is a seriously strong force since this is a powerful combination. Their nature is inscrutable so no one will ever know where they stand with them, let alone what is really on their mind. They're secretive, so they tend not to mind if others are too. People are drawn to them as if by compulsion. They are as alert and clever as the usual Gemini but also have an amazing ability to grasp something without having it explained to them. They are supremely analytical and they use this ability well in their work. They like offices, number-crunching, and being a sleuth. These Geminis are also into their bodies—inside and out. They make good health workers but mostly just enjoy looking after themselves. They'll do their daily jog, take their vitamin supplements, get their acupuncture treatments, then go out and meet the world. If there is one Gemini that comes anywhere near following a routine, it will be the one with Scorpio rising. Everything else might appear rather casual, but in one area, such as following a health regime, they'll run like clockwork.

GEMINI WITH SAGITTARIUS RISING

Relationships are all-important for Gemini with Sagittarius rising, yet finding themselves will be their greatest challenge in life. All Geminis are influenced by the people they come into contact with, but these Geminis suffer from this trait even more and need to be aware of their own unique qualities. Otherwise they may end up projecting their most praiseworthy traits onto someone else. Geminis with Sagittarius rising know how to tell a joke, and this talent should not be underestimated because it makes them great entertainers and people-pleasers! On the other hand, they can be a little outspoken, perhaps even flippant and, as a result, some might call them superficial. If they only live their life through this side of their personality, they may end up leading a somewhat frivolous existence, but Geminis always have another side that cannot be ignored. They are intelligent and amenable human beings who enjoy and benefit from being around other people. They have a tendency to identify with others and when the other person is someone of importance—and that will often be the case since Gemini has such discerning taste—they will profit in some way from the association.

GEMINI WITH CAPRICORN RISING

Don't judge them by the way they look! Geminis with Capricorn rising can come across as a little too intense, but don't be afraid. Underneath the heavy exterior, they're still happy-go-lucky, chatty Geminis.

They're intuitive but also fearful of their own strength so they sometimes appear to be shy, or at least to shirk the limelight. They make great conjurers or psychologists, but their sharp instincts also make them good with finance and the money markets. Any rundown on them would be incomplete without the mention of sex appeal. They are sensual beings and they like to have fun, especially behind closed doors! They're charming creatures whose mere presence tends to turn people on. They have the ability to give one hundred percent of themselves and they are tireless. They can be calculating, which is a good thing, unless they use it purely for their own advantage, which could earn them a bad reputation. However, transformation is a constant theme in their life, so they are adept at turning one thing into another.

GEMINI WITH **AQUARIUS** RISING

〜〜〜 Full of ideas and inspiration, the Gemini with Aquarius rising has a knack for invention. This may turn out to be their career or may just be their way of finding simple solutions to long-standing problems. Aquarius rising enables them to broaden their perspective on life. It gives them the ability to look beyond things, to forgive, and to find answers to their questions. Knowledge and education are their conscious goals; they have a humanitarian streak and dream of making the world a place where peace and love abound, and freedom reigns. However, they may be a little heavy on the intellectual side of these issues and may need to work on the emotional side in order to be fully believed. This is an idealistic combination, but make no mistake, they are still highly persuasive, smooth-talking Geminis beneath the sweetly smiling exterior and, because they are so successful at getting what they want, they'll make good ambassadors, diplomats, lawyers, conciliators, preachers, and judges. They'll also do well in advertising or art. They are very keen on all things foreign and enjoy travel more than the average Gemini. This gives them focus, understanding, and a generous nature.

GEMINI WITH **PISCES** RISING

Family and background have had such an influence on the Gemini with Pisces rising that they'll always try to break free and be their own person. It's natural for everyone to be a product of their environments, which all have something valuable and unique to offer, but it may take these Geminis the greater part of their youth to understand and accept themselves rather than go searching for something they're not. By establishing themselves in their own home and having a place where their authority is not in question, they'll have the feeling of safety and security that they need to thrive. If your average Gemini is multi-faceted, the one with Pisces rising has mega-multi facets! Yes, they are talented, intuitive, and gorgeous people, but it's only when they begin to look within that they find what they are looking for. By investing in property and land, these Geminis can increase their worth. They're also highly artistic, but if they want to find their own unique place in the world, the best place to start will be their own backgrounds, perhaps even their ancestry. This is where they'll find their real treasures.

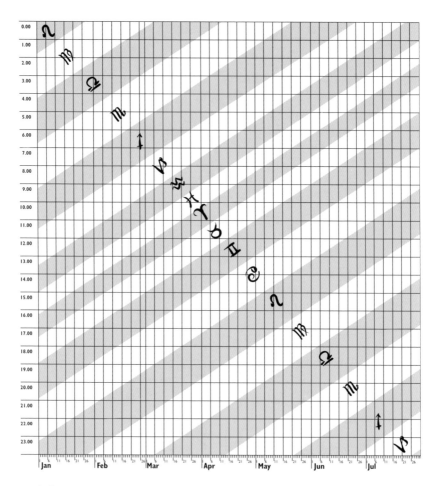

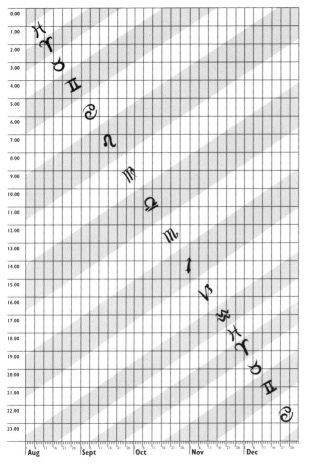

New York
latitude 39N00
meridian 75W00

♈ aries		♎ libra	
♉ taurus		♏ scorpio	
♊ gemini		♐ sagittarius	
♋ cancer		♑ capricorn	
♌ leo		♒ aquarius	
♍ virgo		♓ pisces	

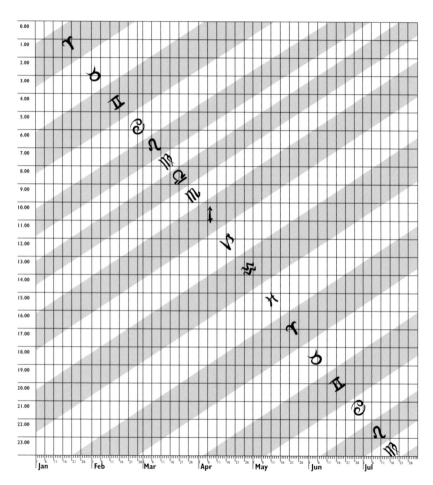

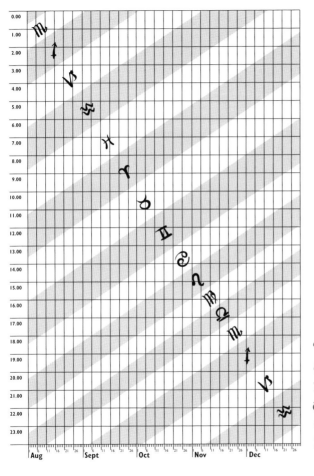

RISING SIGN CHART

Sydney

latitude 34S00
meridian 150E00

♈	aries	♎	libra
♉	taurus	♏	scorpio
♊	gemini	♐	sagittarius
♋	cancer	♑	capricorn
♌	leo	♒	aquarius
♍	virgo	♓	pisces

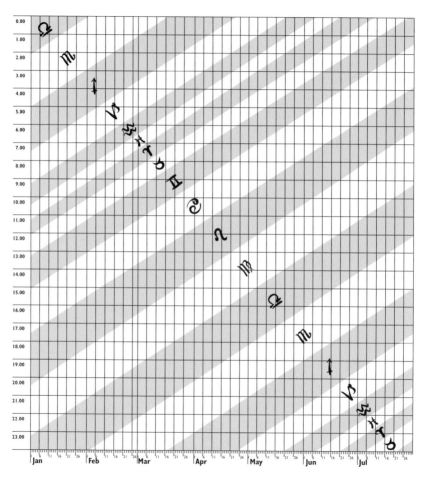

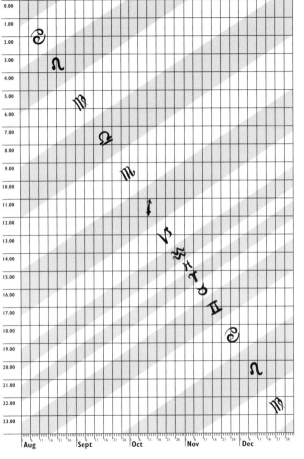

RISING SIGN
CHART

London

latitude 51N30
meridian 0W00

♈	aries	♎	libra
♉	taurus	♏	scorpio
♊	gemini	♐	sagittarius
♋	cancer	♑	capricorn
♌	leo	♒	aquarius
♍	virgo	♓	pisces

PART THREE
RELATIONSHIPS

THE GEMINI FRIEND

A chatty, witty Gemini friend should be mandatory for everybody. Even though their inability to stay still or stick to one opinion, and their unreliable timekeeping drive people crazy, they're also incredibly entertaining and interesting, and unbelievably good fun. Their delightful sense of humor has them on a permanent search for the new, exciting, and downright ridiculous.

Their lightning-quick mental agility and their thirst for information makes them brilliant communicators, always ready, with their eager smile, to offer a fresh perspective. Spend an hour in their company and you'll gain a lot of information, some valuable, some completely useless, but because they make everything sound so engrossing and funny, you'll not know which is which until much later. At the very least, you'll always have a stimulating time.

Geminis get bored of talking to someone long before that person tires of the conversation. Their twinkling eyes frequently scan the room for someone else they can connect with but, in spite of this, always put Geminis at the top of your guest list for any social event. They will mix with everyone, buzzing with enthusiasm and oozing social grace. When they meet other people, their perceptiveness allows them to home in on the most interesting aspects of anybody's character. They can bring shy people out of themselves and can turn extroverts inside out in their search for understanding.

GEMINI WITH **ARIES**

These two are both talkative, witty, and restless. There's always an atmosphere of fun and adventure even if they're only spending the evening in front of the television. Aries delights in the clever, fast-moving intellect of Gemini, while Gemini eagerly gets caught up in the enthusiasm of the fearless Aries. However, when two such high-energy people are together, the excitement has a tendency to spiral out of control. Both are thrill-seekers, neither wanting to miss out on a moment's fun, so exhaustion could be a frequent result of time spent together. Great playmates they may be, but they need time apart to recharge their batteries.

GEMINI WITH **TAURUS**

Taurus's earthy approach can help to ground the airy nature of Gemini, so in this respect they're very good for one another. Gemini's agile, intellectual approach will add another dimension to the Taurus tendency to think only in concrete terms. Taurus can offer the advantages of stability and security, while Gemini provides the fascination of bright, new, and lively conversation. After a while, however, Gemini's flippant behavior and inability to stay still could irritate the Bull, but Gemini's quick thinking usually comes to the rescue before there's any major problem.

GEMINI WITH **GEMINI**

When two Gemini friends get together it's as though they have found their long-lost twin. Finally, here is someone they can relate to, someone who totally understands them and can follow all their verbal leaping about with the same fleet-footed mental agility as they possess. Sure, there will be times when they are both on their own individual trip, chatting simultaneously about completely different things, and then the noise level can become a little irritating. But each understands their friend's need for freedom of expression. All the lighthearted fun they share will be sure to result in constantly high phone bills.

GEMINI WITH **CANCER**

These two make a wonderful comedy double act. They both understand and appreciate the absurdities of life and when they get together, it's as if they are sharing a private joke that the rest of the world just doesn't get. Cancer has a tendency to get a little emotional at times and this may put Gemini in the uncomfortable position of being at a loss for words, just as Gemini may disappoint the Cancer who is in need of sensitivity and sympathy. However, on the whole, they get along well together; the highly intuitive, emotional intelligence of Cancer is offset perfectly by the clever, inventive Gemini mind with its capacity for quick, clear thinking.

GEMINI WITH **LEO**

There is a natural inclination toward friendship between these two. Both recognize their differences in character and appreciate the other all the more for them. Leos delight in buzzy, cheerful Geminis with their ready smiles and rapid-fire astute observations, just as Geminis can't help but be impressed by the good-natured warmth and self-confidence that ooze from their Leo friends. Wherever they go together they make a stunning impact, with Gemini's clever wordplay perfectly complemented by Leo's flashy high drama. They know the entertaining effect they have on others and, what's more, they love it, so repeat performances are guaranteed.

GEMINI WITH **VIRGO**

This is a strange combination in the friendship stakes. They share some common ground and both offer something that the other does not have, yet there is a random quality to their relationship. Mental connection happens easily enough and their conversations are bound to be stimulating, fun, and interesting, but Gemini can lose patience with a Virgo who wants to slow communication down and analyze things more deeply, while Virgo may find the way Gemini constantly changes perspective to be flippant and childish. They'll both enjoy spending time with each other but they're unlikely to be joined at the hip.

GEMINI WITH **LIBRA**

Having fun comes easily to these two. They're like a couple of birds on the wing, swooping and diving around each other in playful flights of fancy. There'll be a plenty of laughter, too, since nobody appreciates the creative turn of phrase in a Gemini joke quite as much as a Libra, and when it comes to expanding the mind, Geminis know that they have found a soul mate in their Libra buddy. When they meet up together it's to have a good chat, so they'll probably spend hours in some favorite lunch spot, ordering endless steaming cups of coffee and solving the problems of the world while giggling at its absurdity.

GEMINI WITH **SCORPIO**

This is an odd couple for friendship. Scorpio is all depth, intensity, and brooding, while Gemini is light and airy and unable—or perhaps unwilling because that would require attention and focus—to reach the same profundity. It would be difficult for these two Sun signs to see eye to eye but, on the other hand, certain planetary influences in their charts could actually make this into a truly productive pairing. Where Gemini has the ideas, Scorpio can see the big picture. Together they could make a storm in a teacup. There is potential here for amazing things.

GEMINI WITH **SAGITTARIUS**

The Twins and the Archer are opposite one another in the zodiac and the result could be one of two things—love or hate. Sagittarius takes the long view while Gemini sees the immediate surroundings. Together they could conquer the world or they could end up walking different paths entirely. Both have a slapstick sense of humor and really know how to have fun. Other people will have to beware as pranks and practical jokes will abound when these two are together. But when they get serious, Sagittarius will probably ignore the lightheartedness of Gemini, which is what makes Gemini tick, and Gemini will dismiss the philosophy according to Sagittarius.

GEMINI WITH **CAPRICORN**

Gemini and Capricorn frolicking down the street together and having a good time will look different at the start of their journey to when they finish. To begin with, they are all smiles and good intentions, though those intentions will differ. Later on, Gemini will be getting impatient waiting for Capricorn to catch up, while Capricorn will be feeling annoyed at being hurried and made to change pace—and then probably slow down deliberately. Capricorn's humor is a little dark for Gemini but, if they are prepared to give it a go, both could learn a lot from this friendship.

GEMINI WITH **AQUARIUS**

Gemini and Aquarius are the ultimate meeting of minds and pairing of friends. These two will have a wonderful time together, but anyone other than another Gemini or Aquarius who tries to get in on the act will feel out of place. Neither of these two deliberately choose to make anyone feel uncomfortable but their vibrational frequency is tuned to one another and to no one else. This is a friendship that could last a lifetime. They understand one another and since, for them, emotions are a foreign language, neither will let them get in the way.

GEMINI WITH **PISCES**

Gemini and Pisces have adaptability and friendliness in common, which could take them a long way as acquaintances. They can get along pretty nicely on a superficial level, but if Pisces attempts to get beneath the surface, as Pisces likes to do, Gemini will become defensive. There aren't many things that unnerve a Gemini, but being unable to use logic to explain the intuitive tendency of a Pisces mind is one, and that's when Gemini can get agitated. However, these two will fascinate one another because, though they have much in common, they also have plenty that is not just different, but totally unrecognizable to the other.

THE **GEMINI WOMAN** IN LOVE

At the start, it's hard to pin a Gemini woman down. She's flighty, flirtatious, and just a little bit fickle. Commitment is a very big thing to ask of her until she's had a good look at all the options. It's just that, with so many potential partners around, and all of them so obviously attracted to her, how can she possibly choose? She'll simply have to spend some time with each to see if they hold her attention for more than an hour. After all, she's very fair.

She's also romantically minded, but because her mind is on a never-ending quest for new and exciting experiences, no one can ever predict when she's going to be in romantic mode. Nor can anyone predict what will put her there. The trigger that does will be visual or verbal rather than physical; she's rarely stimulated by crude, earthy passion unless her interest is also grabbed by some mind-blowing idea. But she will be in romantic mode often, even if to other, slower-thinking people, her idea of romance seems to be just a fleeting fancy.

She has a superb imagination and will create all kinds of fascinating fantasies about love and togetherness, while her manner of expressing them is so sweetly lighthearted that no man will ever feel pressurized by a Gemini girl. But she's not the type to want to work hard at her relationships. If love doesn't flow naturally then it's unlikely to get her juices flowing at all. She doesn't respond to pressure from her lovers either; for her, freedom of action is all-important. And if a lover wants her to pay attention to him, then he had better be saying or doing something really interesting.

When a Gemini woman is in company she'll be floating around a room smiling and laughing and drawing the gaze of any hot-blooded male who wishes to escape from the mundane. Just the spring in her step and the wiggle of her walk seem to promise lightness and fun and, what's more, she'll deliver on that promise. Effervescence and sparkle come so effortlessly to her that even when she's feeling down she won't burden anyone with her problems; she'll just smile, crack a joke, and carry on partying.

But this is where she may create barriers, for the man in her life would feel closer to her if she trusted him enough to talk about her problems. All that witty repartee, vivacious personality, and inability to sit still produce a smokescreen that prevents people from getting too close before she's ready. When she is, however, she offers her partners a loving heart and a sweet nature that is expressed in a myriad of ways. She'll whistle while she works on the domestic chores, so long as nobody expects her to be the drudge all of the time. Then, quick as a flash, she'll be into a challenging, intellectual conversation, running rings around everyone. The next minute, she's heading off to the tennis court where she'll give even a decent player a seriously good workout. The song "I'm Every Woman" was probably written by a Gemini girl!

GEMINI WOMAN WITH **ARIES MAN**

In love: The witty, flirtatious, lighthearted Gemini woman draws the Aries man to her like a bee around a honeypot. She thrills to his energetic masculinity with such obvious delight that she captures and engages his fascinated attention. These two will feel an immediate infatuation with each other and the attraction is powerfully intriguing to both. The intelligent, stimulating conversations that they will indulge in will provide hours of surprise and pleasure. The initial enticement can quite naturally develop into a compelling love, provided the Gemini girl doesn't let her Aries man see her flirting with other men. It's not that she necessarily wants to attract more bees, it's just that her boredom threshold is very low, so she can't help but inject a little bit of excitement into any conversation. However, since the Aries man knows that he is exciting enough for ten women, he quite naturally won't understand. In this relationship, nothing should be taken for granted and expectations must be verbalized. When it comes to commitment, it will need to be spelled out, as both parties enjoy freedom and neither handles rejection well. Whether it lasts forever or not, this will be one of the most memorable experiences of both their lives, and they'll be grateful to have crossed each other's paths. Quantity isn't the issue here: quality is. It's possible for this well-matched couple to go the distance and enjoy the many intimacies that will grow between them as time goes on, but if one of them gives up, they can both call it quits.

In bed: The Aries man is the party that the Gemini woman has been dressing up for all her life and once they find one another, she'll be ready to strip off completely while teasing him mercilessly. There's lots of fooling with this couple! The Gemini woman is capable of making his toes curl with total ecstasy because she can touch and stimulate him intellectually like no other. She spins such a yarn, arousing his imagination and raising his blood pressure until he believes she's a goddess of love walking the earth. She sees him as her inspiring hero and can't wait to run her hands over him. They're both tactile creatures and very fast movers when it comes to sexual expression. She's Air, he's Fire —an essential combination for raising the sexual temperature— so the room may well start smoking and the fire engines may have to be called. This couple should make sure the bed is equipped with a fire blanket, and they should also ensure that those chandeliers are well attached to the ceiling, as they're both into variety!

GEMINI WOMAN WITH **TAURUS MAN**

In love: This relationship starts off rather touch-and-go, so the Gemini woman will feel as though she is in an earthquake—she'll know there's something going on, but won't be quite sure what it is until it has hit. As she finds it so hard to maintain one position for any length of time, there's something about the Taurus man's steadfast, immovable charm that fascinates her. It's hard for her to believe that a human being can be so solid. From where she's standing, he looks like a statue of Adonis! She'll be drawn to him initially because he emanates a powerful masculinity that she could really get into, while he finds the witty, quick-thinking Gemini woman delightful enough to warrant further attention—although he may have trouble following her strange conversation down the twisting turns it sometimes takes. The Taurus man is intrigued by her excitability but can, at times, get a bit heavy in his demand for a simple, no-nonsense approach to life. Then she'll wonder where all the fun went and her light, flirty, and fickle manner can leave him feeling confused about where he stands in her heart. If she slows down and he speeds up so that they meet halfway, then he'll teach her the real meaning of romance and make her feel like a true woman, and she can give him a new perspective on fun and spontaneity.

In bed: The Taurus guy is all about manly strength and direct, no-fuss sexual contact. This won't leave much room for innuendo and intrigue, which are all part of the playful Gemini woman's seductive tool kit. She will always be fascinated by his firm, solid stance, and will never tire of playing with him, it's just that her rules and his don't match up, which could result in two grown people sulking because the other doesn't want to play the game properly! On occasion, and with some persistence, she could build his anticipation up to the point where he's raging with desire. However, the teasing temptress routine—trying to steer him first in this direction and then in that instead of spending a little longer in one place—could simply put him in a rage. He doesn't really like anyone toying with something as serious as his sensual pleasure, and he demands a solid and tangible response to his sexual advances. If he feels there's any doubt she's interested in pursuing an evening of passion, then the Taurus man will probably assume that she's not and will storm off, confused and hurt. The Gemini woman, on the other hand, loves the thrill of not quite knowing what's going to happen—too much certainty takes all the fun out of the moment when two people finally end up wrapped around each other.

GEMINI WOMAN WITH **GEMINI MAN**

In love: These two just love to love one another. Watching the sunrise and listening to the dawn chorus after spending a night together will be a regular form of entertainment for this pair of Twins. They have so much to talk about, so much to laugh about. They'll certainly never run out of things to say, but forgetting the time as they chirp away to each other means that they always end up in a rush, either to catch up on some sleep or to get off to work. They also have an innate understanding of one another's need for some space, and although they'll have separate buddies, they'll also share many friends. If they don't see each other for a few days, they'll miss one another's company badly because together they make a whole, each completing the other. This is such a symbiotic pairing that when they finally get back into each other's arms, or even in one another's vicinity, they breathe an unconscious sigh of relief, as if they have found something that was lost. If they play Twenty Questions, they can get to the 200th question and they'll only just have started. The name of their game is fun and frolicking, but there must always be a serious side to life as well. With two such fun-loving people spurring each other on to ever more dizzying heights of hilarity, the practicalities may fall by the wayside unless one of them decides to play the responsible Twin.

 In bed: "Show me yours and I'll show you mine!" is the teasing cry of one Gemini lover to another. This eternally youthful pair are always inquisitive about each other's minds, bodies, and souls. They enjoy foreplay and afterplay, and all kinds of fooling around. They like to push buttons and see what happens, and will only stop pushing when the response becomes predictable. Innuendoes and double entendre are a constant source of titillation for these two. They enjoy "in jokes," have pet names for each other, make up saucy stories, and can be seen giggling to themselves at almost every opportunity. Every word becomes a turn-on and their sexy banter is never-ending. They may not always be there for one another, but they're always switched on to the other. They'll even put their cell phones on vibrate and call each other for hours! What is more, these two are serious thrill-seekers. Both thrive on variety so the bedroom simply doesn't have the same connotations for them as for other people. They could be inspired to whip off their clothes at any time and be swept along on a hurricane of passion just about anywhere—on a beach, in the elevator, or in the neighbor's tree-house.

GEMINI WOMAN WITH **CANCER MAN**

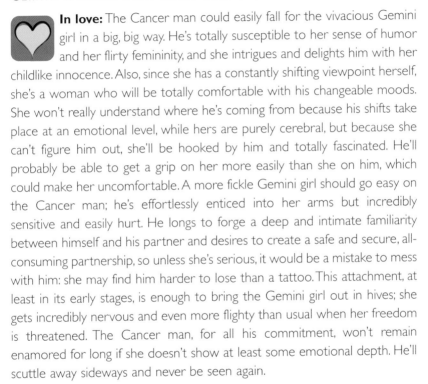 **In love:** The Cancer man could easily fall for the vivacious Gemini girl in a big, big way. He's totally susceptible to her sense of humor and her flirty femininity, and she intrigues and delights him with her childlike innocence. Also, since she has a constantly shifting viewpoint herself, she's a woman who will be totally comfortable with his changeable moods. She won't really understand where he's coming from because his shifts take place at an emotional level, while hers are purely cerebral, but because she can't figure him out, she'll be hooked by him and totally fascinated. He'll probably be able to get a grip on her more easily than she on him, which could make her uncomfortable. A more fickle Gemini girl should go easy on the Cancer man; he's effortlessly enticed into her arms but incredibly sensitive and easily hurt. He longs to forge a deep and intimate familiarity between himself and his partner and desires to create a safe and secure, all-consuming partnership, so unless she's serious, it would be a mistake to mess with him: she may find him harder to lose than a tattoo. This attachment, at least in its early stages, is enough to bring the Gemini girl out in hives; she gets incredibly nervous and even more flighty than usual when her freedom is threatened. The Cancer man, for all his commitment, won't remain enamored for long if she doesn't show at least some emotional depth. He'll scuttle away sideways and never be seen again.

In bed: The Cancer man may look tough, but underneath that hard shell he's as soft as butter. He wants to spend long romantic evenings walking along the seashore and talking his Gemini girl into bed, which is wonderful and really works for her. However, the moment will come during that long walk when her imagination will have been captured, and she'll be ready to cut to the chase. Droning on in that lovey-dovey voice of his will only spoil her excitement. She's running out of patience. She wants him now! If she touches him gently he'll melt into her arms then hold her firmly in his claws. The sexual temperature could rise to boiling point! Her selection of sex toys may frighten the fragile Crab a little, at least until he feels that the relationship is steady and that they're in bed together for the long haul. He's a natural man and doesn't feel the need for any enhancement in order to get her high, or vice versa, but he's accommodating to the needs and wishes of his irresistible Gemini girl. Although these two are essentially different, they're also deliciously compatible because they have so much to discover. All in all, there's plenty of thrilling anticipation.

GEMINI WOMAN WITH **LEO MAN**

In love: The Gemini woman will adore her Leo man and that's just perfect, because he'll adore having her adore him. Winning his favor means that she'll be showered with expensive gifts and treated like a queen. But while she dashes about in her childlike way she must be careful not to let her crown slip, and she certainly can't let her hair down around him as he's rather particular about appearances. There's no question as to who wears the pants in this relationship; the Lion is all man and will thoroughly enjoy being the one who provides and protects. But the Gemini woman is no damsel in distress; she'll pull her own weight but will also manage to make him feel she needs him because, for her, he's one of a kind. She scratches his back, and he'll scratch hers; there's mutual understanding and love here. Meanwhile, he's flashy and showy, with immense pride and a love of glamour and sex appeal—and not just his own but also his leading lady's. Out in the world, where making an impact is so important, the Gemini woman can be the perfect complement to the sophisticated Leo man. Her delightful wit and the graceful way that she trips the light fantastic reflect well on him and inspire him to be at his most generous and indulgent. She will be enthralled by his zesty, feisty character and although he can be rather traditional at times, she, like him, is attracted to all that glitters and is gold. Meanwhile, he's appreciative, very loving, and has a big heart.

In bed: Nothing excites the Leo man quite as much as having the naughty but nice and nymphlike Gemini woman around him. She flutters about like an exotic bird, always remaining just out of reach as he stalks her then pounces. The thrill of the chase appeals as much to her as to him, for she knows how to play this game better than anyone! Once he catches up with her, he'll keep her enthralled and her passion expertly caged in order to release it at precisely the right moment. When she proves herself to be worthy of his regal attentions, he'll have her quivering and begging for more. Meanwhile, the Gemini lady is no simpleton: she's quick when it comes to learning his rules and will run her fingers through his mane and teasingly pleasure him with those delicate but dexterous digits of hers. The dynamics of this couple in bed are way too much for weak-kneed, delicate souls or the fainthearted. Their oscillations between hot and heavy, and light and teasing will spiral into a frenzy of delight and ecstasy. They instinctively know how to wind each other up in the most delicious way until a torrent of tension is released like a rush of lava spewing into the night sky. Hot stuff!

GEMINI WOMAN WITH **VIRGO MAN**

In love: Both Gemini and Virgo are ruled by Mercury, the planet of communication, information, and adaptability, so there will be certain signals passed between the Gemini woman and the Virgo man that others just can't pick up on. Whether these signals have anything to do with love, however, is another thing, though there is a connection, which at least promotes conversation. After a while they could get used to each other's ways of communicating and chances become higher that they'll fall in love. Having been born under an Earth sign, the Virgo man is sensual and sensitive to what moves the Gemini lady. He cherishes her by giving her all his tender loving, but it may be a touch too much. She might not know how to handle herself in the face of so much genuine sentimentality. Sure, he has a sense of humor, but he's serious when it comes to love, while she prefers to make light of the whole thing, even though she is capable of making the Virgo man feel warmly loved. This is a mentally stimulating combination but the Gemini woman will need to practice speaking from the heart rather than the head, and the somewhat practical Virgo man needs to try not to pin her down to one point of view. Celebrating the other's differences while feeling cozy about the mercurial similarities that exist between them is a great start. Once they get the hang of it, the love they make will carry more intensity, warmth, and meaning.

 In bed: They'll both have read all the instruction manuals, from *The Kama Sutra* to the latest kinky stuff. They'll know which bit goes nicely where, and what just causes friction, and as their love grows, the motions will become less mechanical. Mercury is the planetary ruler of both Gemini and Virgo but, unlike all the other planets, Mercury doesn't have a gender, so role reversal is common when the Gemini woman and Virgo man get between the sheets. It doesn't matter who is on top, who comes or goes first, or who is inside or out. When they get tired of one position they can always switch to another. However, Gemini is likely to get bored more quickly than Virgo, and will want to move at dizzying speed through a series of complex poses designed to keep her man excited. But sometimes, the opposite effect is the result, because at the heart of a Virgo man's sexuality is a desire to get to the bottom of things and really understand the workings of each physical sensation. One way of keeping her still while he employs his skills is to whisper a stream of fantastical, titillating possibilities and proposals in her ear. This sort of mental gymnastics will always act as a distraction. And the way for the Gemini lady to keep her Virgo man's attention is to try and indulge him with a little more e-motion, not just the latest motions. He's generous in bed and deserves a lot in return.

GEMINI WOMAN WITH **LIBRA MAN**

 In love: When the Gemini woman and Libra man get together, a magical thing happens: they present each other's best side to the rest of the world. They'll be on everyone's A-list for dinner parties because together they are the pinnacle of sophistication, refined taste, beauty, charm, and wit. Their conversation flows with intelligence and articulation. Mentally, they just click; they've really got it. There's lots of laughing and loving, jesting and teasing between them, and the world just seems a lighter, brighter place when they are around. When they are alone together all the magic is turned on the other. The Gemini woman is helplessly seduced by the elegant, eloquent, clever Libra brain—he can romance her with just a look and a word—while she will intrigue and impress him with her quick-thinking ability to grasp all his serious conceptual ideas, and will constantly surprise him with her amusing, playful banter. The only problem that these two face is that they both find it practically impossible to make up their minds on almost anything. But that's alright because they love each other's company so much and have all the time in the world to decide on whether they should buy this sofa or that, live here or there, or go north or south on vacation. But, once they've made a decision, they'll grow old together and never tire of one another. This is certainly one of those matches that are made in heaven. Life will be eternal bliss.

 In bed: For this couple, bed is their playground. It's where they'll linger on into the early hours with the most artful, tasteful, and romantic lovemaking ever. The Libra man really thrills when all his senses are tingling with desire. He adores the feel of beautiful lace against delicate silken sheets and he's a man who'll appreciate the natural softness of his Gemini lady. But he'll also buy the necessary accessories to play up her coquettish beauty—perfumed candles, scent, romantic music—and complete the perfect lovemaking. These two both like to talk and it would amuse the rest of the world if they could hear the running commentary during one of their marathon sex sessions. What the Gemini woman has to say would go down well at any late-night risqué comedy club, while her Libra man could make a small fortune in the romantic greeting cards business. But these two are unlikely ever to write their material down because they're so caught up in just being together. Each time they glance at one another, excitement flutters in their hearts, their breathing gathers pace, and everything feels fresh and new, just like the first thrilling time they came together. Born under the sign of the Scales, the Libra man knows how to get the balance right and is ever aware of the importance of sharing and the nature of give and take. These fanciful, romantic lovers will have each other reeling in ecstasy.

GEMINI WOMAN WITH **SCORPIO MAN**

In love: At first, the Scorpio man might be tempted to write off the Gemini woman as a delicate, amusing, but rather shallow female. And he'd be worried—and with good reason—that he might not be able to hold her attention long enough to form the intimate bond that he so craves. She may be blind to his more attractive qualities, since any attempts at flirting with him only encourage his penetrating inspection, and this sends her flitting nervously away before she can really get to know him. If she treats him as a fleeting curiosity then she'll find that it's his attention that wanders first, which is something this girl is simply not used to. He will, of course, want the physicality that she can offer and will even be attracted by the energetic way she moves about the room. He also has the gall to believe that he knows her every thought, but, in fact, this isn't so far from the truth. Meanwhile, the Gemini woman might find the Scorpio man a little scary at first, with his intense way of looking at her and his brooding manner. She'll feel as if he's going to eat her up, and he might do if she's lucky! If she takes her time and can settle her nerves while this predatory man is putting her under the microscope, she'll find him as compelling as an erotic novel. If he knows what's good for him, he'll learn to mind his manners and allow this love to grow. It might just stand the test of time and mature rather nicely.

In bed: When it comes to sex, the last thing this guy wants is a bit of lighthearted slap and tickle. For him, achieving deep and meaningful satisfaction is absolutely crucial. He doesn't mind the adjustment period that she'll need in order to adapt to his zealous sexual style. This phase can provoke some passionate gestures from him and some strong statements from her about limits. To him there's nothing like feelings being aired to fire up his already brooding libido, but this won't necessarily be a turn-on for her. However, at the mere thought of having her, he can turn into a keen, mean, loving machine in a matter of seconds, and that's difficult for any woman to resist. He'll happily indulge his Gemini girl's desires by involving himself fully in the employment of her collection of erotic toys, but should she ever seem to prefer them to him, then his sexual jealousy knows no bounds. If the Scorpio man ever suspects that his Gemini woman is about to change her mind about him, that's sure to put him in a gloomy mood. She'll have to change her address and phone number because Scorpio never forgives or forgets. But she'll have turned him on as never before!

Gemini woman with **SAGITTARIUS man**

In love: This is a case of "opposites attract." She's all about finding diversity and he's searching for a unifying theme. Together they'll be deep into endless debate, lively conversation, challenging mental gymnastics, and practical jokes. The Gemini woman can't help but love the Sagittarius guy. She finds the intellectual expansion that comes from spending time with him a powerful incitement to love. She can't possibly fall for anyone who doesn't turn her on mentally, and since this guy doesn't just turn her on, but also turns her inside out and upside down as well, she'll tumble straight into his arms. He watches her with an Archer's eye, delighting in the challenge she presents. She never reveals a target he can pin her down to for very long, but if anyone can nail her, he will. They're a match, that's for sure, fitting together like a hand in a glove. Even when one gets irritable and wants some space, the other won't hesitate to allow it and will back off graciously. Neither is clingy or possessive, and both need their space so will respect the other's need; they'll each just go and explore another landscape but wouldn't dream of questioning the other's loyalty—well, at least not beyond normal expectations. They have different motivations, but similar intentions. He'll make her laugh until she cries, but that just fuels her exhilaration. As they dance around each other, their feelings will be woven into a pattern of love that touches the very fabric of their souls.

In bed: Whooaaa! Bring along the riding crop and giddy-up! Need we say more? Talk about insatiable appetites! No one would believe what goes on behind this couple's closed doors. Their antics would leave anyone watching either in a state of shocked disbelief or feeling inspired to spice up their own love life. What they'd see wouldn't really be any more lewd than average, it's just that the raucous, sometimes acrobatic, burlesque revelry that goes on while these two are making love is truly amazing! The Sagittarius man, for all his high-minded ideals, still has enough of the wild animal about him to teach his Gemini lover to unleash the fantasies that she never knew she had. Her planetary ruler, Mercury, has wings on his feet, but nothing could prepare her for the sexual terrain she can cover riding on a Centaur. He'll take her to heaven and back again. She's a nimble little minx, though, and can stay with him through all their athletic exertions for as long as he can keep it up. He'll love her thighs so stockings are a prerequisite, and if she squeezes his flanks between them, he'll happily submit to her directions. These two not only adore one another in a romantic sense, they also have amazing fun.

GEMINI WOMAN WITH **CAPRICORN MAN**

In love: The Capricorn man is an old soul so if the Gemini girl is into father figures, there's great scope for her here. He could look after her for life and takes the responsibility of caring for fragile little creatures very seriously. That's alright with her up to a point, but she's not as fragile as all that and needs him to be a playmate at least some of the time. She won't like being scolded like a child when all she wants to do is indulge in a bit of frivolous fun. If she's got a masochistic streak, then she'll have met her match. He's heavy, intense, and brooding; she's lighthearted, cheerful, and flirtatious. That isn't to say that they're entirely incompatible. Everyone has their moments and if these are coordinated, they could hit it off. If they both get most of their mental stimulus outside of the relationship, from work, family, and friends, they could find the nest they create together rather refreshing. And there are instances when their dissimilarities are a good thing, for instance when it comes to humor. The Gemini girl is quick and witty enough to grasp his sense of irony and satire and bounce it straight back, to the delight of both. Her youthful zest enlivens his low-key, somber habits, but some attempts to lighten him up, particularly when he is under the shadow of a cold, dark mood, will just irritate him and in response he'll put a chill around her heart that will have her picking icicles off for weeks.

In bed: The old soul and the young at heart can be an exciting combination when they get together between the sheets. When the man in her bed is a stuffy, self-controlled Capricorn, she relishes the challenge to intrigue and seduce him. Not that it takes much of an effort; he's really into physical pursuits, and sex is his favorite. He knows exactly how to bring his Gemini lady to an ecstatic high, and she will never tire of the way he unflaggingly indulges her. Nothing brings out the kid in a Goat quite like the prospect of sexual tomfoolery. She may have to warm her hands in order to arouse his deeper passions, and this could take longer than she's used to, but the more time he can spend stringing out the sexual experience, the better it is as far as he's concerned. For him, making love is a serious business, but he's renowned for his stamina, so the Gemini girl should prepare herself for a long, long night. Once he carries her to his peak, rest assured there's no free-fall drop. He'll hold on tight and take her down the scenic route.

GEMINI WOMAN WITH **AQUARIUS MAN**

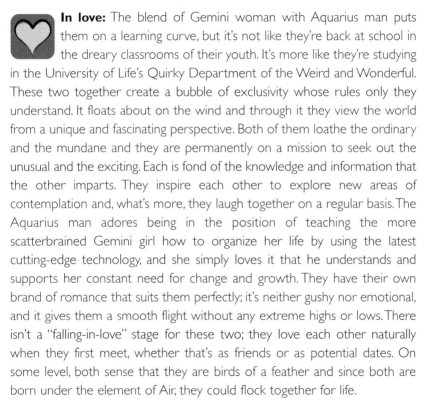

In love: The blend of Gemini woman with Aquarius man puts them on a learning curve, but it's not like they're back at school in the dreary classrooms of their youth. It's more like they're studying in the University of Life's Quirky Department of the Weird and Wonderful. These two together create a bubble of exclusivity whose rules only they understand. It floats about on the wind and through it they view the world from a unique and fascinating perspective. Both of them loathe the ordinary and the mundane and they are permanently on a mission to seek out the unusual and the exciting. Each is fond of the knowledge and information that the other imparts. They inspire each other to explore new areas of contemplation and, what's more, they laugh together on a regular basis. The Aquarius man adores being in the position of teaching the more scatterbrained Gemini girl how to organize her life by using the latest cutting-edge technology, and she simply loves it that he understands and supports her constant need for change and growth. They have their own brand of romance that suits them perfectly; it's neither gushy nor emotional, and it gives them a smooth flight without any extreme highs or lows. There isn't a "falling-in-love" stage for these two; they love each other naturally when they first meet, whether that's as friends or as potential dates. On some level, both sense that they are birds of a feather and since both are born under the element of Air, they could flock together for life.

In bed: The Aquarius man and Gemini woman never run the risk of becoming bored when it comes to sex. Because they have so much in common, they feel as if they've known each other for a lifetime so they trust one another when it comes to experimentation. And experimentation rules with them, so anyone who thinks they're the first to try it in a particular place or position will probably find that the Aquarius man and Gemini woman have already tried it. This couple are founding members of the Mile-High Club, yet that's not what lies at the root of this relationship. They like to mix it up a bit in the sexual sense, and with both being so keen on all that's new and exciting, they allow their limitless imaginations free rein in order to invent original ways of bringing each other pleasure. Funny how they both feel safe in something strange and new, but that's because of their tight (and not just emotional) bond. Aquarians love to defy expectation, even to shock on occasion, and since nobody loves a surprise or catches on as quickly as a Gemini, it's sheer pleasure all the way for both of them. There are no dark corners or perplexing motivations in this relationship; just pure electricity to light up their libidos.

GEMINI WOMAN WITH PISCES MAN

In love: Once their boundaries are clearly defined so there's no room for any misunderstanding, the Pisces man will mystify his Gemini lady as much as she will bamboozle him. A bizarre fascination can grow between these two as they sense that in this relationship they have found someone who understands their need for fluidity and spontaneity. It doesn't seem to matter much that they express that need in completely different ways. The Pisces man feels his way through life and while he appears to be confused, he's really just waiting for the right moment to move closer to his Gemini woman—or to swim away. Her fluidity is the result of her never-ending stream of thought about whether or not she fancies being with him. Sometimes she does and sometimes she doesn't. He'll commit sooner than she will, but one of his problems is his keenness to bare his soul to her too soon. This appeals to the Gemini lady and she could get hooked, but they should both try to assess the reality of the relationship before immersing themselves fully. They're both very changeable, but once they've decided to align themselves, they will have put together an apparently ideal partnership. Keeping up appearances may be a little more of a challenge, since there will be times when both will be blowing about at sea and will long for the other to provide directions or a safe harbor. That's when they could lose each other and simply drift out of each other's reach and they'll never be completely sure how they got swept so far apart.

In bed: If, with her twin-cam, speedboat mind the Gemini girl can fathom the depths of the Fish and doesn't confuse him too much in the process, together they could create the ideal fantasy of man, woman, and more! These two are highly attracted to each other sexually and know instinctively that they could steam up a bedroom together. And they will, at least once, because they are equally and powerfully drawn by the other's enchanting sex appeal. However, when the experience is over, neither should be too surprised if the other has slipped away. The Pisces man is pursuing an emotional as well as a physical connection with a lover. He wants to feel her pleasure and won't be satisfied with her simply telling him what a good time she's having. And her constant sexy banter may even distract him and put him off his stroke, especially if there's the slightest hint of insincerity. He himself is unlikely to be honest about what bugs him. The Gemini woman, on the other hand, needs to know that not just his body is engaged in their coming together. His silence could unnerve her; all she needs is some assurance or even just a squeak of approval. This liaison will kick-start itself, but uncertainty on both sides could lead to it fizzling rather than sizzling.

THE GEMINI MAN IN LOVE

The Gemini man is a real charmer—appealing and incredibly romantic and masculine. He has a lot to give, but consistency, safety, and security won't be among his offerings. Since he's a master of language and communication, he could melt even the iciest woman's heart with his poetic declarations of eternal love. He's worth his weight in gold when it comes to saying the right thing, but his words speak louder than his actions, which is something she should remember, particularly if he fails to turn up for the next date! But he knows he's good at stringing the right words together, and will always be able to talk his way out of trouble. Like all Geminis, he has at least two sides to him, so the next time his lady sees him and is feeling romantic, she may find he's not in the same space. In fact, he could be a little distant. If he does fall for one woman—which can happen even though commitment is a dirty word—he'll be loyal, despite what some people say about Gemini's dualistic, cheating nature. Sure, he's an incurable flirt and can be in love with more than one person at a time, but he'll only have faithful romantic intentions toward one of them. And it's true that he likes variety, but once he has decided to stay with one lucky lady, he stays. He is trustworthy and wants to be trusted, but he needs space and likes the company of his other female friends. He tends not to be suspicious, jealous, or possessive and, indeed, doesn't really comprehend such emotions, so he'll have little patience for anyone who feels that way toward him. His partner needs to accept that, if he finds anyone with something interesting to say, he'll want to discuss it with them, whether that person looks like a fashion model or a bag lady. His ideal woman will have a rational, slightly detached manner, and will titillate his brain with her interesting conversation. Of course, she must also be interested in him so if she asks robotic questions about his day or dismisses his interests as "man stuff," he'll quickly realize that she's not really into him. Many women fall for him but, unless he's declared that he's smitten too, it could be a heartbreaking experience. Until he's sure of himself, he could go either way. If his date starts making plans for the future, he'll disappear extremely swiftly. Obviously it's impossible to control the yearnings of the heart, but this man needs a little challenge—nothing too difficult but enough to make him feel he has to try to win his woman. Above all else, he prefers a woman who'll offer him a good intellectual challenge. Mental stimulus is what keeps a relationship with this man alive, though, of course, amazing lovemaking would be a tasty bonus. But even in bed, a Gemini man likes to have his mind tickled as much as the rest of his body.

GEMINI MAN WITH **ARIES WOMAN**

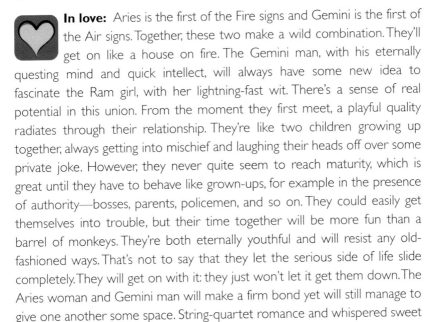 **In love:** Aries is the first of the Fire signs and Gemini is the first of the Air signs. Together, these two make a wild combination. They'll get on like a house on fire. The Gemini man, with his eternally questing mind and quick intellect, will always have some new idea to fascinate the Ram girl, with her lightning-fast wit. There's a sense of real potential in this union. From the moment they first meet, a playful quality radiates through their relationship. They're like two children growing up together, always getting into mischief and laughing their heads off over some private joke. However, they never quite seem to reach maturity, which is great until they have to behave like grown-ups, for example in the presence of authority—bosses, parents, policemen, and so on. They could easily get themselves into trouble, but their time together will be more fun than a barrel of monkeys. They're both eternally youthful and will resist any old-fashioned ways. That's not to say that they let the serious side of life slide completely. They will get on with it: they just won't let it get them down. The Aries woman and Gemini man will make a firm bond yet will still manage to give one another some space. String-quartet romance and whispered sweet nothings are unlikely to be heard often, if at all. Instead, lively conversation and silly jokes will create a constant babble of noise.

In bed: The Aries woman is clever but so is the Gemini man and he'll have talked his way into her bed before she's even realized what's happened. Or, if she did realize, she let him do it anyway because she so enjoys the entertainment. Geminis are entertaining and unpredictable lovers, and they are rarely ever boring when they get between the sheets, which should be enough to satisfy any Aries girl's thirst for novelty. She'll be fascinated with the Gemini man's ability to flit from one pleasure zone to another, constantly surprising her with his unusual rhythms. He will adore her pure, uncompromising passion and the enthusiasm with which she responds to his artful ministrations. Geminis are known for their wandering minds, but an Aries woman won't give him the chance to think about anything else while she single-mindedly pursues the satisfaction of her sexual appetites. The only place his mind will be wandering when he's with her is in and around her body. They're a fantastic match. Gemini is great with his hands and she'll definitely let his fingers do the walking—all over her body! With his flowing energy and skillful lovemaking, he'll be the only person the Aries woman will ever wait for, while she knows exactly how to wind her Gemini man up to the point of frenzy.

GEMINI MAN WITH **TAURUS WOMAN**

 In love: This is not an impossible love match, but a Taurus woman will probably expect a lot more from her partner than a Gemini man can give. Gemini and Taurus appear to be like chalk and cheese, but these two signs are next to one another in the zodiac, which indicates that they could have more in common than meets the eye. If there is a spark between them, it will be very special indeed. The Taurus woman's earthy approach can help to ground the airy nature of the Gemini man, and his whimsical cheerfulness will no doubt introduce some new and exciting elements to her life. He's impressed by her sense of beauty and creativity, and she delights in his witty conversation. The Gemini man's constant flow of ideas will always add a fresh dimension to the Taurus woman's tendency to think in concrete terms. In this respect they are good for one another and they make a colorful, dynamic couple. The question is: Will the Taurus woman's enduring patience eventually wear thin when all she wants to do is relax, while Gemini man wants to satisfy his untiring thirst for new people, places, and things? In Gemini talk, the answer is "yes" or, perhaps, "no." With Gemini, things can chop and change unless they have a pact between them. In the language of a Taurus, this means "commitment," but that's a word which could be interpreted in a myriad of ways by the Gemini man.

 In bed: The Gemini man certainly knows a thing or two about variety and if he can apply this to his Taurus woman, then she'll make him feel more than man enough in return. Meanwhile, the Taurus woman could probably teach any Tantric sex practitioner a few things about endurance and holding back. When she applies this knowledge to her Gemini man, she can bring him to a truly intense level of toe-curling ecstasy. Between the sheets, on the dining-room table, or out in the yard in the open air, the Taurus woman has a lot to offer the Gemini man, and if she can hold his attention for long enough, he'll be immensely grateful for the earth-moving pleasure that she gives. He needs as much mental stimulation as physical to get him vibrating at the right frequency to give her sexual pleasure. On the other hand, the Gemini man will appeal to the Taurus woman's imagination, allowing her to lie back while he gets her going with his fantastic tales of love and lust. However, he's such a social butterfly that when he flutters around a room chatting with whichever pretty thing catches his attention, it's likely to be her jealousy rather than her passion that he arouses. If their romance is still intact once the reality of his flirtatious behavior meets her intransigent possessive streak, they'll both end up glowing with smug pride.

GEMINI MAN WITH **GEMINI WOMAN**

See pages 57–58.

GEMINI MAN WITH **CANCER WOMAN**

In love: The Gemini man has the ability to set off the Cancer woman's intrigue radar simply by walking into the room. She finds him attractive and lovable, and intuitively knows what makes him tick. It amuses her to see his childlike enthusiasm in action, and the stories he tells make her imagination work overtime. Her beguiling femininity simply spurs him on to try to capture her attention even more. He'll make her laugh—and cry. He's a marathon talker, so she'll always know what he's thinking, but he doesn't speak about his feelings as much as she'd like. Although she has a certain amount of intuition, she can only be aware of what he's feeling some of the time. She could teach him a thing or two about expressing his feelings, but he may tire of hearing what she has to say on the subject because it gets a little too close to the bone for his liking. He doesn't know how to handle such matters unless he takes things very slowly, one step at a time. Meanwhile the Gemini man may be able to teach her about less intense human relationships. He's got lots of friends and knows how to surf on the crest of life, but he may only ever skim the surface of her emotions, setting off ripples that excite her but never move her deep down. If it feels good, they should go for it, but they'll need to learn to express their feelings in a way that both can understand.

 In bed: The Gemini man is into tickling and teasing with fingertips and feathers. Even when she takes the initiative—which she'll do frequently—he seems to be in charge and is never short of a new game to play or a different place to try out a new technique, whether on her body or in some new location. He'll drive his Cancer lover mad with so much pleasurable foreplay that, as he takes her to the brink over and over again, she might even discover a demanding, impatient, and pleading side to her sexual persona. He's got a wicked sense of fun and she'll enjoy lying back and watching with amusement as he scampers all over her body, drawing responses from erogenous zones that she didn't know she had until she met him. She wants to be able to pleasure him as much as he does her, but his dexterous skill and playful imagination seem to fill all the gaps. It excites him to see the effect he can have on this enchanting woman. Next to his boundless energy and enthusiasm, she may begin to feel inadequate, though needlessly so. She has to learn simply to accept his gift of pleasure; after all, he thoroughly enjoys offering it. But for all his clever skills, the amusing fun and games only touch her superficially. This Cancer lady could soon feel frustrated in her desire for a more intense emotional relationship.

GEMINI MAN WITH **LEO WOMAN**

 In love: She's picking up good vibrations from the flirty Gemini man while he ups the energy level of conversation and love around her. The big-hearted Leo woman has a generous laugh and his quick wit will give her plenty of opportunity to spend it freely. There'll be many a playful moment in this relationship as she enjoys seeing his response to her good-humored teasing. He'll fall at her feet and offer up his heart the moment she radiates that famous warmth of hers in his direction because, of course, just being in this regal lady's company is a privilege. He feels honored and flattered by his ability to bring a sunny smile to her face. These two are natural friends and will give each other plenty of latitude to express their unique individuality without compromising, but compromising is really essential when it comes to a Gemini man and Leo woman. There will be the odd occasion when his lighthearted manner can seem to her to be somewhat lightweight, and when her powerful personality and dynamism could completely overwhelm his more fragile ego. She is demanding and he can be flaky, and the more demanding she gets, the flakier he becomes, unless a line is drawn and they both agree on a limit. With so much admiration and respect for one another, agreeing on a limit is something that they should easily be able to do. This love match holds massive potential as long as both are aware of their own occasionally challenging behavior, and as long as they keep up the lavish demonstrations of affection.

 In bed: The passion and heat that the Leo woman can generate in the bedroom will inflame this man until he's like a firework on a clear night. Once Lady Lion gets hot, she burns with lustful desire and is almost too hot for words, but a Gemini man can handle her. He will delight and excite her but this freedom-loving Gemini man is not the type to cage this lioness in. He'll be expert at lighting her touch-paper and fanning her into a raging, rampant wanton, but he may find that he's got more than he bargained for. If he then behaves a little timid and nervous, it's only because lion taming is not what he's trained for. She could make a meal of him, which, it's readily apparent, is a massive turn-on, but eating him all in one go just makes her hungrier still. He could probably use some instruction and no one could teach a Gemini man how to honor his sexual promises better than a Leo woman. She'll be delighted by his willingness and he'll love her need for him.

GEMINI MAN WITH **VIRGO WOMAN**

In love: Conversations with a Gemini man give the Virgo woman a real buzz; she'll be impressed by his rhetoric and clever observations. He'll arouse her interest so that she'll be lured into wanting deeper and more meaningful conversation. She's met her mental match; his intelligence is equal to hers, though somewhat different in nature. He finds her obvious interest in him flattering and reassuring, and if the two of them can maintain this level of adoration, that will keep them going. But while the two of them are, mentally speaking, busy little bees, he has a tendency to show off, buzzing about from one subject to another and perhaps becoming as irritating as a wasp. And he can be just like that in the love department, too—all buzz and no substance. Though laughter should flow easily between them, she'll never quite get him to explore the emotional side of their relationship with the depth that she desires. For the Gemini man, conversations that cater to a Virgo woman's need for everything to be analyzed in minute detail are like sticky fly paper. They only serve to make him frantic to pursue his freedom, which has the effect of making her jittery. With all that nervous energy bouncing back and forth between them, the relationship won't feel very comfortable. Unless they're both willing to work at it, once they've flitted, fluttered, and buzzed around each other for a while, it won't be long before one of them just buzzes off permanently.

In bed: Because she is totally into his sense of humor and is highly attracted to the quick and easy way that he communicates, the Gemini man could lure the Virgo woman giggling all the way to the bedroom. Laughter is a powerful aphrodisiac and when these two get together, it just seems so natural. He fascinates her and encourages her sexual urges so that all she wants to do is to get to know him more intimately. However, once they're lying side by side and ready for some loving, he doesn't quite know what to do with her. Perhaps he'll whisper fantasies in her ear and tease her a little, and then she might do the same for him. Each has a similar seduction technique for getting the other into bed and, predictably, this could get a little boring for the Gemini man, which means that the Virgo lady will once again find her man lacking in substance. In the end, for her at least, fantasies only work when there's a bit of flesh attached to them. The Gemini man will definitely connect mentally with his Virgo lover, but on a physical level the bits don't fit so smoothly. However, both do have a brilliant capacity for creativity and they could easily arouse one another's sexual appetite by introducing an element of surprise. If the love is there, the drive to make a more meaningful physical relationship will be there, too. Together these two could forge a strong love that will sustain many erotic nights of passion.

GEMINI MAN WITH **LIBRA WOMAN**

In love: The Gemini man and Libra woman will be flitting around each other like a couple of hummingbirds looking for, and finding, sweet nectar. Both delight in being around someone who possesses the same bright and airy approach to life as they do. The Libra woman, who loves to make a mental connection, will never run out of things to say to Mr. Gemini, and he'll hang on her every word. Many a dawn will break before either of them tire of their scintillating conversations, although, because they are so much on the same wavelength, there will also be times when words won't be necessary. It's true that the erratic and restless Gemini could throw Lady Libra's world out of balance, but she finds his energy so irresistible that somehow it doesn't seem to matter that much to her. An uncertain future with him is better than a future without him. The practicalities of life will definitely get in the way of their bliss but time apart will only make their longing and love for one another grow. Her effortless grace, elegance, and charm captivate and hold this man's normally wandering attention, so he'll no longer have such a great need to do his own thing, at least not without his Libra woman by his side. She brings out his desire to create something magical for the both of them. There is such a natural affinity between the Libra woman and Gemini man that they'll never be seriously distracted when in each other's company. There's lots of honey where this relationship comes from.

In bed: When a Libra woman tells a Gemini man her sexual fantasies, he thrills at the way they reflect his own and will do everything in his power to indulge her and make them real. Even if he doesn't quite get it right, they'll both end up giggling and rolling around the bedroom so much that lovemaking will be a truly joyous event. When he brushes his dexterous fingers over her body, she exudes a soft sweetness that is an exquisite invitation for him to do more, go farther, and fly higher. Both of them have a vision in their mind of the ideal romantic union expressed in a sexy, sensual storm that sweeps them along on the wings of erotic passion. The unbearable lightness of being that can exist when these two wrap their bodies around each other brings them closer to that vision than either could hope for. The climactic moment is often reached at the same time, and together they will float high in the divine light of heavenly bliss. The Gemini man excels at propelling his Libra lady into these stratospheres of pleasure and she'll stay with him all the way, while she brings him higher than he ever thought possible. Such is the strength of this loving union that they easily become one, which is a major feat for the dualistic Gemini man. There will undoubtedly be some pitfalls, however. Sooner or later, one or both of these lovers will have to get out of bed and get dressed if they are to pay the bills.

GEMINI MAN WITH **SCORPIO WOMAN**

 In love: There may be an initial attraction when Gemini man meets Scorpio woman. He certainly does have some very engaging qualities and appreciates her obvious sexuality. It is also possible that because they see things from such a different perspective, they may be able to give each other a whole new way of looking at life. But, fundamentally, they are as different as chalk and cheese. If they ever agree on anything it will be a miracle! She'll find it very hard work creating the depth of intimacy she's after with him, and he may find her possessiveness and intensity a little too restricting. Miss Scorpio wants to be totally sure that the bond between them is unbreakable, but that only makes Mr. Gemini behave even more erratically and he may turn and fly, which is exactly the opposite of what she wants. Is it any wonder that they end up viewing each other with a certain amount of suspicion? In most cases, then, this isn't likely to be a long and happy union, unless, of course, other factors in their horoscopes indicate a strong compatibility. For example, he might be one of those unusual Gemini men who are more trousers than talk, and she could be one of those very rare Scorpio ladies who will allow her man a long leash. On the surface there isn't much to recommend the relationship for either of them, but look beyond that and there might just be some miraculous tie that ends up holding them together.

In bed: The Scorpio woman is unlikely to want more from the Gemini man than a one-night stand, and vice versa. It'll be fun while it lasts, and will give them both a good temporary fix, but after that, the only thing that might keep them attracted is those devilishly tempting one-night stands. Neither party could ever turn one down. She's a very sexy girl with a powerful desire to lure a man into a fathomless pit of passion, but he's usually just too lightweight for her. However, his playful antics could just tease her into joining him, as he is sometimes too naughty for her to resist. For the Gemini man, all that sexual intensity is a little suffocating; he needs to be able to breathe and see what's going on. At best they'll make a habit of replaying that first encounter, which is a highly engaging prospect. At worst, she'll be thinking about how soon she can begin faking an orgasm and getting the guy to fly away home.

GEMINI MAN WITH **SAGITTARIUS WOMAN**

In love: Excitement and adventure meet and meld in the Gemini man and Sagittarius woman relationship. Nothing is ever dull when the two of them are together. They can make anything fun, even an argument! Whether they're chatting in a café, dancing till dawn, or making love on a beach, they just know that their partner is enjoying it as much as they are. They're opposites who exert a fatal attraction on each other. Here is a woman who can give the freedom-loving Gemini man a taste of his own medicine. She leads an active life and follows her own interests with a singular intent. She's warm and generous and would embrace the idea of him joining her at any time, but he shouldn't expect her to hang around and beg him to get involved. That's what he'll love about her; she takes life as it comes. More often than not he'll want to join her on her spontaneous adventures and invite her along on his, so these two will often be found trucking around together, laughter ringing out and music blaring. They can travel optimistically through life, never letting its more serious side get them down. And as they'll never get bored with each other, it's unlikely either will find a good reason to finish it. Such a great relationship is hard to find, especially for two such free spirits. Even if they do wander away from one another, it won't be too far or for too long.

 In bed: The Sagittarius woman will love the way the Gemini man quivers when she touches him and, knowing how quickly her passionate energy gets going, he'll become transfixed as he dances his fingers all over her bare skin. And so it goes both ways with these two. Both enjoy constant stimulation—mental, spiritual, and physical. Making love is a highly charged experience that will leave their bodies fulfilled and tingling with cosmic love. With her insatiable adventurous spirit, the Sagittarius woman will enjoy exploring Gemini man's body: he's totally responsive as she discovers previously uncharted territory. And this is one woman who isn't afraid to boldly go where no woman has gone before; she's uncannily accurate in her guesses as to what will get the Gemini man's sexual energy going. It's as though his thoughts and desires fly like arrows straight into her mind. As a Lady Archer, she knows just how to handle the arrow of lovemaking and is well practiced at hitting the bullseye. He, on the other hand, knows how to feed her fire so she can keep climbing to the peak, but he does chatter so, which can be a little distracting, so she might have to climb all night to reach the summit. But there's so much sexual energy between these two that they might as well be going at it throughout the night. It's near impossible for them to keep their hands off one another, even while asleep!

GEMINI MAN WITH **CAPRICORN WOMAN**

In love: The Gemini man can bring out the playful side of the Capricorn woman, while the Capricorn woman can bring out a more stable side in the Gemini man. It's not often that she meets someone who can shake the heaviness out of her spirit, and it's just as rare that he meets someone who can make him feel so close to settling down. His light, happy sense of humor is highly infectious, and he appreciates it when she is able to put her intensity into words. Both have a need to laugh at the absurdity of life, and as long as the jokes keep coming, then they'll keep the relationship going. However, Gemini can sometimes appear too flaky for Lady Capricorn's more practical approach to life; she knows the value of a good idea, but has little time for endless ingenuity unless she can see him putting it into action. He'll be impressed by her aspiring soul but gets impatient with her need to create a sturdy staircase to carry her upward when he can just sprout wings and fly. It doesn't seem to matter to him that he'll only ever make fleeting visits to the summit. Though she takes longer to get there, once she does she'll have a permanent place to stand, high above everyone else. In some way, these two make a perfect partnership. Each has something the other lacks and, deep down, they really do admire one another for it.

In bed: The Gemini man is a chatterbox, in the bedroom as much as anywhere else, so the trick for the Capricorn woman is to stop him talking and get him touching. Although she appreciates his need to make a big mental "thing" about their lovemaking, and will patiently indulge him, it can get a bit frustrating waiting around while he builds himself up. By the time he gets going, she'll be almost there but, as a Capricorn, she'll be able to pace herself. She's a very physical woman and longs to feel him get up close and personal with her. She could certainly help him along by reading him some erotic poems or stories—and that's the perfect foreplay for a Gemini man filled with sexual fantasies. But he always likes to feel he has an escape route, which is why, even when all he wants to do is swoop and dive on his Capricorn lover, he'll pretend that this is the last thing on his mind. When, of course, he does it, it will take her by surprise, but without the steady buildup that she needs, it could all be over before she's halfway to the climax. This is where her ability to take charge and her firm grasp come in handy. The only problem is that he finds this so intensely erotic that he might end up falling over the edge before she can catch him!

GEMINI MAN WITH **AQUARIUS WOMAN**

 In love: What a delightful couple the Gemini man and Aquarius woman make. They say that "time flies when you're having fun." If that's the case, then these two will be old and gray before they know it! Life for them will just hurtle along at a breathtaking pace in an exciting blur of love and laughter. They'll spend many a night chatting and chirping away like a couple of lovebirds in spring. But it won't all be lightweight, frivolous banter; these two will get into such seemingly way-out, seriously mind-expanding, philosophical discussions that they'll believe they're the first ever to travel this intellectual terrain. Although they can be very much in love, they would never be seen canoodling in the corner of a subway car or on a bus. They're far too busy chatting away. Both are capable of writing beautiful romantic poetry and they often do, even in the little notes and text messages they send to one another. Theirs is the kind of love that doesn't need constant demonstration. The only problem that could undermine this near-perfect relationship is that the Gemini man can be evasive and the Aquarius woman can be detached. This makes developing the relationship into something more than friendship a little hit-or-miss in the early stages, but once they fall in love, they'll realize what a valuable commodity they possess, and with all their fun and laughter, they'll be rich beyond measure.

In bed: Physical love between a Gemini man and an Aquarius woman is a breathtaking experience—full of surprise and wonder. She has a few tricks up her sleeve, not least because she's amazingly inventive and can be relied upon to come up with some very original ways of capturing the Gemini man's attention. She's quite unlike anyone he's known before. Some would say that she's a kinky kind of lover. With her alternative spin on every possible position, her antics will definitely fire him up! She'll be his ultimate spine-tingling experience, and she'll love how he loves it. He's a playful lover so she should feel no embarrassment in getting out the toys. If she hasn't already acquired any, then a trip to the toy store will be a stimulating and hilariously sexy outing for them both. They make a great team; the Aquarius woman's very definitely his match in the game of verbal foreplay. When these two jump into bed together there's a mutual feeling that here is someone with whom they can be truly free. Their sexual prowess is not going to be marked on any score card, so they can abandon any hang-ups or performance anxiety they might have. The result is truly fantastic and sensually thrilling!

GEMINI MAN WITH PISCES WOMAN

In love: The Gemini man and Pisces woman appear to float and flow around each other in a delightful dance. They both like to look at life in a variety of ways; his thoughts are lateral while hers have depth, so together they've got all the moves covered. She intrigues and confuses him, which he finds a devastatingly appealing combination. He's always good fun to have around and loves a puzzle, particularly one that's as mystifying as the Pisces woman, but unless he's able to figure her out, at least partially, he could get distracted by something that is more logical and more understandable. In her view he somehow appears flippant and superficial; his words suggest understanding but his actions lack conviction. Her super-sensitivity can make him feel as though he's walking on eggshells and that, for a man who usually trips through life lightly, is rather nerve-racking, so something in this pairing will never quite click. Neither of them should dive into this relationship headfirst; it might be wiser just to paddle about until something better comes along. It all depends on whether they're both prepared to make a continual effort, but it's unlikely that either of them could stay in the relationship for long unless the Gemini man can stay silent and tune into her depth of feeling, at least long enough to get into her and into the experience of really making love. The other option is for the Pisces woman to adapt to his constant need to verbalize, and just savor her moments alone when she can enjoy some peace.

 In bed: There's an instant sexual attraction between these two, but it has a quizzical quality rather than a rampant, passionate one. Just about anything inspires the curiosity of the Gemini man. Both of them feel the thrill of possibility, and that can be enough of an aphrodisiac to get them as far as the bedroom. Once there, the Pisces woman could really tickle his fancy. He adores her flowing sensuality, her inspired touch, and the way that she drifts dreamily into his arms, but the Gemini man is more likely to get off from hearing her sexual fantasies than from actually making them come true. It's probable that her fantasies would raise rather more than just the hairs on his back, but she won't want to divulge her secrets to someone who might not be around for long. Sounds like a bit of a disappointment? Maybe, but he's also very clever and agile and might sweep down on her without any prior warning. And when that happens, he'll prove to her how talented he really is.